PONY
CARE

Written by Joanne Bednall

The publisher would like to thank the following for their
kind permission to reproduce their photographs:

Bob Langrish, Ray Moller, Peter Chadwick, Kit Houghton,
Andy Crawford, Neil Fletcher, Tim Ridley, Andrew McRobb.

Appaloosa, Golden Nugget, Sally Chaplin (photographed by Stephen Oliver);
Hanoverian, Défilante, Barry Mawdsley, European Horse Enterprises, Berks;
Exmoor, Blackthorn Piccottee, Mrs Carter, Wilton, Wilts;
Highland, Fruick of Dykes, Countess of Swindon;
Connemara, Spinway Bright Morning, Miss S Hodgkins, Spinway Stud, Oxon;
Shetland, Chatsworth Belle, Mrs Hampton, Briar Stud, Herts;
Thoroughbred, Ardent Lodger, Mr & Mrs P Duffy, Pencein Stud, Clwyd;
Andalucian, Campeanero XXIV, Nigel Oliver, Singleborough Stud, Herts;
Lipizzaner, Siglavy Szella, John Goddard Fernwick & Lyn Moran, Ausden Stud, Dyfed;
Fjord, Ausden Svejk, John Goddard Fernwick & Lyn Moran, Ausden Stud, Dyfed;
Saddlebred, Kinda Kostly, Kentucky Horse Park, USA;
Quarter Horse, Doc's Maharajah, Harold Bush, Kentucky Horse Park, USA;
Falabella, Barley Sugar, Lady Fisher, Heathfield, East Sussex;
Budyonny, Reactive, Pearl of Switzerland Trade Association, Moscow, Russia;
Caspian, Hopstone Shabdiz, Mrs Scott, Henden Caspian Stud, Wilts;
Arab, Cavu the Prophet, Don & Jo Ann Holson, Cavu Arabians, Sanger Texus, USA

A Funfax Book
First published in Great Britain by Funfax Ltd.,
an imprint of Dorling Kindersley Limited,
9 Henrietta Street, London WC2E 8PS
Copyright © 1999 Funfax Ltd.

A PONY OF YOUR OWN

Owning a pony is a huge responsibility. All that mucking out, grooming, feeding and worry when your pony's ill, not to mention the huge dent in your family's bank balance, will make you wonder if it's all worthwhile.

True Test
While your friends are out on the town, soaking up the sun on holiday or buying new clothes, be prepared for a sore bottom, muddy wellies and having to mend the rip in your pony's new rug. If you can shrug this off, you're the perfect pony owner!

Miles of Smiles
Trudging through the snow before school to check on your four-footed friend will seem a distant memory once the warm weather arrives. You'll find nothing beats hacking through stunning countryside on a summer's day or winning a rosette at the local show. Yes – owning or looking after a pony is definitely worth it!

PONIES GALORE

Honesty is the best policy. If you can't provide a pony with the care, comfort and attention he deserves, don't buy one. Many pony-mad people haven't enough money, time, experience, knowledge or proper facilities for a pony. But all is not lost – there's always loaning, sharing or working for rides instead.

Twice as Nice
If you have a reliable, pony-mad friend, why not consider sharing? All the costs – a pony, tack, vet's fees and shoes – are halved.

The Loan Arranger
Loaning saves you the expense of buying a pony and tack, but you'll need to pay the owner every week or month in return. Get an agreement drawn up to avoid arguments.

Work For Rides
If you're not lucky enough to live near a riding school or livery yard, you could place an advert in the local newspaper or post office window offering to help out with a horse or pony.

KEEPING A PONY

Ponies need a lot of looking after. Deciding how yours will be kept depends on the facilities in your area – not all of us have the luxury of owning a nice paddock and a stable.

One option is to rent a field with a shelter, another is to place the pony 'at livery'. This is when you share facilities with other people and their ponies at a yard, and pay rent in return.

Grass Livery
This is when your pony lives out. If he's a hardy, native type, it shouldn't be a problem, as long as his field is spacious and has shelter.

Part Livery
Some of the work is done by you (probably after school and at weekends), while the rest is the responsibility of the yard's staff.

Working Livery
If your yard gives riding lessons, this is an excellent way to keep costs down. Your pony pays his way by being used in the school.

Full Livery
This is when everything is provided by the yard. It's by far the most expensive!

THE FIELD

Ponies prefer grazing with a herd than being stuck in a stable, but that doesn't mean you can leave your pony in the paddock and forget about him. He must still be checked at least twice a day and his surroundings examined regularly.

Room with a View
Your pony's field should, ideally, be away from main roads and footpaths. It must be big enough – at least one acre per pony – and have good drainage.

Star Grazing
Perfect paddocks have good grazing; they don't have lots of weeds and muddy or cracked land (this would make a field 'horse sick'). You should pick up droppings regularly and provide clean water in a trough.

Mind the Gap
Ensure that your pony has a shed, hedges or trees for shelter. The fence or hedge surrounding his field must be solid, with no gaps or holes. Gates should be easy to undo (but use a padlock to deter thieves!).

> **Danger!**
> Get rid of litter and poisonous plants instantly.

PONY CARE

5

THE STABLE

Even if your pony lives outdoors, there are times when he will thank you for having a stable. If he's ill, injured or lame, or if the weather is particularly harsh, a stable, or stall (below), will provide a comfortable shelter.

Breath Easy
A stable should have good ventilation so that the air can circulate. This is vital for ponies who cough.

Topping Up
It's important that your pony has a deep bed so he can lie down comfortably. You will need to muck out several times a day, fill his bucket with clean water and keep his haynet full.

Boredom Breaker
Ponies get bored easily. If your pony can see other animals or people, he'll be less likely to pick up bad habits such as weaving (swaying his head from side-to-side), windsucking (grabbing hold of something with his mouth and inhaling air) and crib-biting. Try to leave a radio on if the yard is quiet. Tying a turnip or a ball on a piece of string to a beam will also go down well at playtime!

SAFETY AND SECURITY

You need to follow a few sensible rules to protect both yourself and your four-footed friend.

Horse Sense

Ponies can be panicked by the slightest thing, so use your common sense. Wear a hard hat and gloves, and ask for help with a strong or difficult pony.

Spick and Span

Keep your yard tidy and safe. Sweep up hay and straw, and store mucking out tools carefully after use. Always secure the feed room door from greedy ponies! Human and equine first-aid kits should be within easy reach.

PONY CARE

Field Marshal

As well as picking up sharp objects from your pony's field, learn to spot poisonous plants and remove them. The ten most dangerous are:

- yew
- laburnum
- hemlock
- foxglove
- deadly nightshade
- ragwort
- acorns/oak leaves
- horsetails
- bracken
- privet

Deadly nightshade

Ragwort

Acorns

Yew

Stop Thief!

Deter thieves by:

- freeze-marking your pony
- postcoding tack
- chaining tack to a saddle horse or locking it away
- padlocking the tack room door

MUCKING OUT

Mucking out may be a dirty chore, but someone has to do it...at least three times a day! If your pony is left standing on soiled bedding for long periods, his breathing and hooves will suffer. Bad stable management can lead to a smelly foot disease called thrush.

Snug as a Bug

A deep, clean bed keeps a pony warm, encourages him to lie down and soaks up the wet. There are four main types of bedding:

- straw (wheat is best as your pony is less likely to eat it!)
- wood shavings (better for ponies with an allergy to hay and straw)
- shredded paper
- rubber matting

Tools of the Trade

You will need the following items to muck out properly:

Broom

Shovel

Four-pronged fork

Wheelbarrow

Muck skip

Wellington boots

Shavings fork

Rubber gloves

Rake   Pitchfork   Hose pipe

8

HOW TO MUCK OUT

Mucking out is easy when you know how. Most yards use the 'deep-litter' method which saves time, energy and money.

- Remove droppings with a four-pronged fork. Put them into a wheelbarrow. Toss the clean straw that's left round the sides of the stable. Fork out the dirty bedding underneath into the wheelbarrow and take it to the muck heap.

- Sweep the remaining bits of bedding to the sides. Once the floor is dry, add clean straw. Heap it round the sides to protect your pony's legs and make it deep enough for him to lie down and roll.

Skipping Out
A 'skip out' is a quick muck out. Use rubber gloves or a four-pronged fork to pick up your pony's droppings and drop them into a plastic basket. Top up the bed with clean, fresh straw.

Spring Clean
Several times a year your pony's stable should be completely cleaned out. Wash and disinfect the floor.

CATCHING A PONY

Ponies have to be caught so that they can be checked over, groomed and ridden. Walk up to your pony quietly – flapping your arms and shouting will drive him away.

Direct Action

Approach his shoulder so that he can see you coming. Give him a pat and talk to him quietly before slipping the rope of the headcollar around his neck. Place the noseband over his nose, then pass the headpiece behind his ears and buckle it up.

Hard to Catch
Some ponies refuse to be caught. The trick is to let yours come to you, rather than chasing him round the field for hours.

Tricks of the Trade
Hide the headcollar behind you and hold out a titbit (the sound of sweet wrappers is enough to get most ponies' attention!). Failing that, catch your pony's best friend and bring him in. Yours may feel lonely and want to follow.

PONY CARE

10

LEADING A PONY

Once you've caught your pony, learn to lead him correctly. Walk on his near (left) side with your right hand holding the leadrope by his headcollar, and your left hand holding the other end of the rope.

Turning Out

Lead your pony a good way into his field before turning him to face the closed gate. That way, he's less likely to kick you if he gallops off. Unbuckle his headcollar and gently slip it off.

PONY CARE

All Tied Up

When tying up your pony, attach the end of his leadrope to a loop of breakable string or twine tied to a metal ring. This will stop your pony hurting himself if he tries hard to pull away.

In a Knot

Always tie up ponies using a quick-release knot for safety. Slip the free end of the rope through the string before bending it in an 'S' shape and slotting the rope back through the loop you've just made.

This may sound complicated, but practise makes perfect!

GROOMING

Grooming tones muscles, cleans skin and improves the appearance of stable-kept ponies. Brushing off dried mud helps to prevent the tack from rubbing, too. You should give your pony a good groom every day unless he lives out in winter, when he'll need the grease in his coat for protection.

Tool Box

Your grooming kit should include:

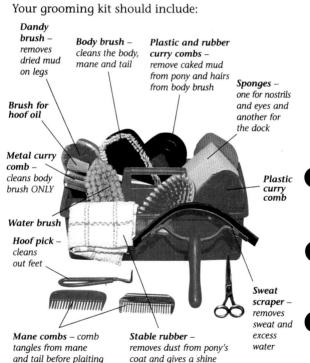

Dandy brush – removes dried mud on legs

Body brush – cleans the body, mane and tail

Plastic and rubber curry combs – remove caked mud from pony and hairs from body brush

Sponges – one for nostrils and eyes and another for the dock

Brush for hoof oil

Metal curry comb – cleans body brush ONLY

Plastic curry comb

Water brush

Hoof pick – cleans out feet

Sweat scraper – removes sweat and excess water

Mane combs – comb tangles from mane and tail before plaiting

Stable rubber – removes dust from pony's coat and gives a shine

HOW TO GROOM

Here's how to clean your pony from top to toe:

Feet First
Facing your pony's tail, run your hand down his leg and lift each foot in turn. Use the hoof pick from heel to toe to remove stones and dirt.

Body Matters
Use the body brush in long, sweeping strokes until you have groomed the whole pony, including his legs. Every few strokes, draw the brush across a metal curry comb to clean it.

Tail End
Hold your pony's tail so the hairs fan down, then run the body brush through them before tackling the mane. Use the water brush to flatten any hairs that stick up.

Sponge Down
Use a damp sponge to clean around your pony's tail (dock). Then use another sponge to wipe his eyes. Rinse before cleaning his nostrils.

Rub it Out
Finally, dampen the stable rubber and wipe it over your pony's coat, leaving it dust-free and super-clean.

FEEDING

Ponies are designed to eat grass, but because we want them to work, we have to provide other foods to boost their energy. It's important never to experiment with your pony's diet without expert help because it could lead to him developing a nasty tummy ache (colic).

Feeding Time
Different types of 'hard' feed can be mixed together according to your pony's type and the amount of work he does. Alternatively, feed a balanced diet of coarse mix or pony nuts.

Sugar beet – ALWAYS soak for 24 hours before feeding

Fruit and roots – ponies love carrots (always slice lengthways), apples and root vegetables

Coarse mix – includes oats, barley and maize

Maize – high in energy, low in protein

Oats – provide lots of energy

Bran – comes from wheat

Chaff – chopped hay (sometimes with oat straw)

Linseed – ALWAYS boil first

Barley – good for your pony's condition

Pony nuts – a general feed

14

FEEDING RULES

DO:

- feed little and often – ponies have small, sensitive stomachs.

- provide a constant supply of clean, fresh water.

- give plenty of hay, especially in winter when grass has little nourishment.

- feed according to your pony's size, temperament and workload.

- provide fruit and root vegetables every day.

- introduce changes to his diet gradually.

DON'T:

- exercise your pony less than an hour and a half after feeding him.

- allow buckets and scoops to get clogged up with dried food and dirt.

- leave lids off feed bins (you'll attract rats).

- feed bad quality forage.

- vary your feeding time – ponies prefer routine.

Added Extras

To ensure that your pony has a healthy diet, he should also be given supplements, including vitamins and minerals, cod liver oil, garlic, limestone flour, molasses and salt.

Here are a few equine illnesses to watch out for.

Off Colour

A poorly pony has a stiff, rough coat and dull eyes. He'll probably stand on his own with his head down, looking miserable and not eating.

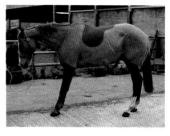

Laminitis

A pony with laminitis (above) has eaten too much rich grass or hard food and he's not had enough exercise. Affected ponies stand with their painful forefeet stuck out in front of them.

Thrush

This is a smelly disease affecting the V-shaped horn (frog) under the pony's hoof. It's caused by bad stable management.

Colic

Colic is an equine stomach ache which can be mild or fatal. The wrong kind of food (such as grass cuttings) or too much food is often to blame.

Lameness

A stone in the hoof, a strained tendon or *navicular* (a serious foot disease) can cause a pony to become lame.

Sweet Itch

Some ponies are allergic to midge bites and will rub their mane and tail raw.

PONY CARE

A PONY'S WELLBEING

Happy, healthy ponies have normal appetites, bright eyes and smooth, glowing coats. Your pony's temperature should be around 37.8-38.5° C (100-101.5°F), his pulse should beat 35-40 times a minute and his respiration at rest should be 8-12 breaths a minute.

Health Hazards

Your pony should stay in tiptop condition if you follow these rules:

- Check him regularly so that you can act quickly if he's off colour.
- Provide him with shelter from harsh weather.
- Feed him a balanced diet.
- Ward off parasites by worming him every six to eight weeks.
- Protect him from insects in summer by applying fly repellent.
- Have him vaccinated against equine flu and tetanus once a year.
- Ask your vet or a horse dentist to regularly rasp rough edges on your pony's teeth.
- Book the farrier every six weeks to trim your pony's feet and fit new shoes if needed.

FIRST AID

Ponies are prone to picking up minor injuries such as scrapes and knocks to their legs. These can be treated by yourself with the help of an experienced adult.

Box of Tricks

You should keep a fully-equipped first-aid kit to hand. All these items are available from your vet or saddler:

- large animal thermometer for taking your pony's temperature
- cotton wool for cleaning wounds
- veterinary Gamgee dressing
- waterproof tape for holding bandages or dressings in place
- a cold gel pack (such as Koolpak) for muscle strains and injuries
- blunt-ended scissors for cutting tape or hair from around a wound
- salt to make up a saline solution for cleaning wounds
- Elastoplast bandages for securing dressings
- flexible cohesive bandages (such as Vetwrap) to keep dressings in place and provide protection
- low-adhesive Melolin pads for cushioning wounds
- antiseptic solution for preventing infection
- antibiotic gel, powder or spray to stop further infection and speed up healing
- Vaseline

TACK

You must have certain equipment to ride a pony. His 'tack' is usually made of leather. It consists of a saddle with a girth and stirrups, and a bridle with reins and a bit.

PONY CARE

Saddle Sense

Saddles suit different disciplines: racing, endurance, side-saddle, showing, dressage, showjumping and Western. But if your pony is an all-rounder, or if you prefer hacking, a general purpose saddle will do. A saddle should be expertly fitted and be comfortable for both pony and rider.

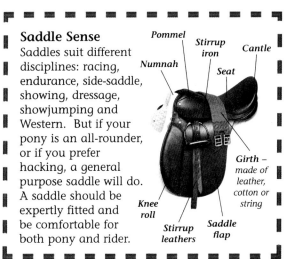

Pommel
Stirrup iron
Cantle
Numnah
Seat
Knee roll
Girth – made of leather, cotton or string
Stirrup leathers
Saddle flap

Bridle Baffler

A bridle and bit enable you to control your pony. A simple snaffle bit is best, although strong ponies are often ridden in a *pelham* or a *kimblewick*.

Odds and Ends:

- Boots (brushing and overreach)
- Martingale – for controlling the head

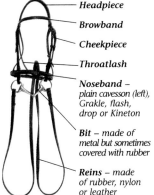

Headpiece
Browband
Cheekpiece
Throatlash
Noseband – plain cavesson (left), Grakle, flash, drop or Kineton
Bit – made of metal but sometimes covered with rubber
Reins – made of rubber, nylon or leather

TACKING UP

Tacking up a pony gets easier with practise. Ask for help if you get in a muddle.

Head First

Tie your pony's headcollar around his neck. Check the bridle's throatlash and noseband are undone. Hold the headpiece in your left hand and place the reins over your pony's head with your right hand. Pass this hand under his jaw and hold the cheekpieces against his nose. Guide the bit into his mouth with your left hand. Place his ears under the headpiece, pulling his forelock over the browband. Fasten the throatlash and noseband.

Saddle Up

Approach the pony from his left (near) side, holding the saddle and numnah in the crook of your arm. Slide the saddle into position, checking the numnah isn't folded up underneath. Let the girth down gently on the pony's off (right) side. Go round to the near side, reach for the girth and buckle it up.

CLEANING TACK

Tack will last for a long time if you look after it. Dirty, cracked leather can be dangerous and uncomfortable for you and your pony.

Elbow Grease

To keep your saddle and bridle in good shape, they should be cleaned after use. First, take the numnah, girth and stirrups off your saddle and the bit off your bridle. While the stirrup irons and bit soak in water, rub over the saddle with a damp sponge to remove mud and grease. Now dip saddle soap into water before rubbing it over a dry sponge. Work the soap into the saddle.

Sleek Finish

Clean your bridle in the same way. Only take it apart if you know how to put it back together again! Once in a while, treat your tack to some leather oil to keep it supple. While it's okay to use metal polish on stirrup irons, NEVER apply it to your pony's bit.

RUGS

Rugs keep your pony snug in his stable, warm and dry in winter and clean and cool in summer.

Rugging Up
In winter, if your pony is an Arab or Thoroughbred type, or if he's been clipped, he'll need to be rugged up indoors and outside.

No Fly Zone
A summer sheet is used in hot weather to keep irritating insects and dust off a groomed pony.

No Sweat
A sweat sheet is like a huge string vest. It dries a pony after a bath, or stops him from sweating if used under a rug.

Winter Warmer
Waterproof New Zealand rugs protect ponies that are turned out in cold, wet weather.

Warm as Toast
Stable rugs (below) are made from jute (a strong fibre), wool or nylon, and they are worn in winter by clipped, stabled ponies.

CLIPPING

PONY CARE

Imagine running a mile in a fur coat and not being allowed to take it off. That's what it's like for ponies ridden in their thick winter coats.

Cut Above

Clipping not only prevents a pony from getting sweaty quickly and losing condition, but it makes him feel more comfortable. Ask an expert.

Clip On

Choosing a clip depends on your pony's workload and lifestyle.

Bib clip: for ponies who are ridden lightly. Just the hair from under the neck and tummy is removed.

Trace clip: good for ponies who are worked several times a week. Hair from the lower part of the neck and sides is clipped.

Blanket clip: leaves hair on the pony's back and quarters. It's perfect for ponies who are ridden every day.

Hunter clip: reserved for hard-working competition ponies. Hair is left under the saddle and on the legs.

HACKING OUT

If you're competent in the saddle, a relaxing ride varies a pony's routine and keeps him interested.

Be Prepared
Never ride alone and always wear reflective and fluorescent clothing – whatever the time of year. Tell a responsible adult where you're going, and take a mobile phone or some coins with you for peace of mind.

PONY CARE

Emergency Measures
Carry some identification – your name, address and phone number – in case there's an accident. Remember to take some baler twine with you for tying up your pony, and a hoof pick to extract stones from his feet.

Good Manners
Never ride on private land without permission. Bridleways, woods and edges of fields are okay, but always remember to close gates behind you.

Watch Out!
Stay alert for low branches, tree roots and logs. Allow your pony to pick his own way through shallow water – avoid deep streams and rivers. Don't allow him to gallop off!

ROAD SAFETY

Only use the roads if you're a confident rider and your pony is one hundred per cent in traffic.

Road Rules

Brush up on your Highway Code. NEVER leave home without wearing a hard hat – it's against the law for under-14s to ride on UK roads without protective headgear.

Sign Language
Learn to signal your intentions clearly to other road users.

PONY CARE

Turning Left or Right
Before you turn, look around for other traffic. Then put your reins into one hand and signal with the other. Hold your left or right arm out straight until you've made the turn.

Slowing Down
Extend your arm and wave it slowly up and down.

Stopping
Hold up your hand to warn oncoming road users.
Turn slightly in the saddle to signal to drivers behind you.

Saying Thanks
Nod your head or put up your hand to thank drivers who slow down.

SHOW PREPARATION

Before an event, brush up on your skills. Practise plaiting, schooling movements and jumping tricky obstacles. If your pony's prone to travelling badly, get him used to the horsebox or trailer.

Wash and Go
If the weather's warm, wash your pony the day before the show and leave a light rug on him overnight to keep him clean.

Perfect Plaits
Plait his mane and tail on the morning of the show. Split his mane into sections. Plait them then roll the plaits up into little knots. Use a needle and thread or rubber bands to secure the knots.

Tips For the Top
- Ensure your clothes are clean, even down to the soles of your boots!
- Your pony's tack should sparkle, too.
- Chalk covers blemishes on white markings and grey ponies.
- Boot polish masks marks on black ponies.
- A dash of hoof oil can make all the difference.

SHOW TIME

Shows are exciting. There are plenty of classes to enter, from clear round showjumping and best turned-out horse, to handy pony and gymkhana games.

First Things First

Allow plenty of time to get to the show. On arrival, organise your pony and his gear, then go to the secretary's tent to collect your number. Before a showjumping class, walk the course so that you can memorise your route and turns.

Take it Easy
Put your pony first. If it's hot, stand him in the shade and ensure he has a bucket of cool, clean water. Don't keep asking him to go in the ring time and time again – he'll soon get tired and make mistakes.

Be Considerate
Don't hog the practice fence, and lend a hand picking up poles once you've finished competing.

Winning Isn't Always Everything!
Reward your pony with a pat or titbit if he's done well.

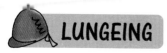

LUNGEING

Lungeing is another way of exercising your pony. You stand still while he moves around you attached to a lunge rein.

Why Lunge?
Lungeing is good for building up a pony's muscles. It helps with his balance and rhythm, and teaches him to be obedient. Lungeing can also be used to correct bad habits and settle an overenthusiastic pony before he's ridden.

PONY CARE

Dressed For Success
In order to lunge your pony, you should wear a hard hat, gloves and boots.

Gearing Up
You can lunge your pony with or without his saddle. Ensure his stirrups are removed or run up their leathers and secure. Alternatively, use a special roller. This is a wide, padded girth with D-rings. Other essentials are a *lunge cavesson* (like a bridle minus the bit and reins, with rings on the noseband), side reins, lunge whip and lunge rein.

HOW TO LUNGE

Organise the lunge rein into tidy loops before you start, or you'll get in a real mess! Attach the lunge rein to the middle ring on the cavesson. If you are lungeing on the left rein, hold the spare rein and whip in your right hand so that your left hand is free to feed out or gather in the rein.

Smart Moves

Stand level with your pony's shoulder and send him away by saying "walk on". Flick the whip towards the ground – not your pony – to back up your command. To increase the pace, say "trot on". If you want him to slow down or stop, say "wa-alk" or "whoa-oh".

> ### Long and Short of It
> Ask your pony to shorten and lengthen his stride by moving in small, then large circles.

Lesson Lingo

Lunge lessons can improve your position, while lungeing a friend will show you how your pony moves with a rider aboard.

LESSON TIME

Controlling your pony, listening to instructions, concentrating on your position and keeping an eye on everyone else is a lot to think about! As you become a better rider, you'll find that it gets easier.

Keep Your Distance

When riding in a school or *manège* (an outdoor ring), remember to leave at least a pony's length between your pony's nose and the tail of the pony in front.

Lead On

The pony at the front of the ride is called 'leading file'. He sets the pace and speed. The slowest pony usually goes at the back.

Fancy Footwork

Arenas are marked with the letters A, K, F, H, C, M and B. Learn where these markers are so that you can ask your pony to perform certain exercises. These include changing the rein (going in another direction), 10- and 20-metre circles, and figures-of-eight.

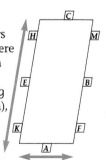

 # EXERCISES

Exercises in the saddle are good for your balance, fitness, confidence and suppleness. Ask a friend to hold your pony's head while you attempt them.

Round the World
This move is quite tricky! Take both feet out of the stirrups and swing your right leg over the pony's neck so that you're sitting sideways. Face the pony's tail before completing a 360° turn.

Touching Your Toes
Touch your right toe with your left hand and your left toe with your right hand. No moving your feet – that's cheating!

Leaning Back
Fold your arms across your chest and lean back until you're resting your head on the pony's quarters. Keep those legs and feet still!

Touching the Tail
Twist in the saddle and touch your pony's tail.

Leaning Forwards
Stand in your stirrups slightly so that you can touch your pony's ears.

Trunk Twists
Swing your arms from side to side.

Reach For the Sky
Really stretch those arms upwards.

PONY CARE

DON'T FORGET!

Use this check-list to jog your memory.
Tick off in pencil each task as you complete it.

Ring the vet to arrange:

Equine flu jab .... ☐

Tetanus jab .... ☐

Teeth rasping .... ☐

Worming .... ☐

Ring farrier to:

Trim feet .... ☐

Fit new shoes .... ☐

Clean tack .... ☐

Muck out .... ☐

Sweep yard .... ☐

Stock up on feed .... ☐

Order hay/bedding .... ☐

Book riding lesson .... ☑

Clear droppings from field .... ☐

Check field for litter
sharp objects/ poisonous plants .... ☐

Repair/clean rugs .... ☐

Fill in show entry forms .... ☐

Pay livery fees .... ☐

Clip pony .... ☐

PONY CARE